FOGGY BOTTOM

BOTTOM

········ *and the* ········

WEST END

For Emily, whose
grandfather taught her
to love history.
From her friend,
Josh Olsen

FOGGY BOTTOM
BOTTOM
·········· and the ··········
WEST END

MATTHEW B. GILMORE
& JOSHUA OLSEN

Charleston | London

THE
History
PRESS

Published by The History Press
Charleston, SC 29403
www.historypress.net

First published 2010

Manufactured in the United States

ISBN 978.1.59629.332.8

Library of Congress Cataloging-in-Publication Data

Gilmore, Matthew.
Foggy Bottom and the West End / Matthew Gilmore and Joshua Olsen.
p. cm.
Includes bibliographical references.
ISBN 978-1-59629-332-8
1. Foggy Bottom (Washington, D.C.)--History. 2. West End (Washington, D.C.)--History.
3. Foggy Bottom (Washington, D.C.)--Pictorial works. 4. West End (Washington, D.C.)--
Pictorial works. 5. Washington (D.C.)--History. 6. Washington (D.C.)--History--Pictorial
works. I. Olsen, Joshua. II. Title.
F202.F64G55 2010
975.3--dc22
2010031403

Notice: The information in this book is true and complete to the best of our knowledge. It is offered without guarantee on the part of the authors or The History Press. The authors and The History Press disclaim all liability in connection with the use of this book.

CONTENTS

INTRODUCTION

Foggy Bottom and the West End are Washington, D.C., in microcosm. Almost every aspect of Washington's history, culture and development may be seen in these two neighborhoods lying between the White House, Rock Creek and the Potomac River.

The land on which Foggy Bottom and the West End now sit was early considered central to the development of Washington. As the capital city grew, they emerged from a cluster of shipping and manufacturing businesses to include all types of residences, from working-class row homes to mansions. Businesses and local institutions went from being small to occupying entire blocks. Urban renewal and highways eventually reshaped large portions of the neighborhood. And the ever-present government grew from a military outpost on a hill overlooking the marshy edge of the Potomac to occupy the entire southern portion of the neighborhood, with one result being that "Foggy Bottom" is now a common way to refer to the U.S. State Department. These same forces and trends also had an impact on the city as a whole, and thus an examination of Foggy Bottom is an examination of Washington.

The history of Foggy Bottom and the West End goes back to the beginning of the nation's capital. The land that these neighborhoods occupy lies adjacent to the port town of Georgetown. Foggy Bottom would share the waterfront and eventually the Chesapeake and Ohio Canal with that community, but first a paper town, Hamburgh, covered much of the area. Thomas Jefferson, in his sketch map of his vision of the proposed capital, located the city primarily in Hamburgh and along the nearby banks of Goose (Tiber) Creek.

Peter Charles L'Enfant's plan, approved by President Washington, spanned a far greater area, stretching to the Anacostia. Hamburgh was merely a small corner—but an important one with access to the water, a major thoroughfare (Pennsylvania Avenue) and land set aside for a park (Washington Circle). Early development was very mixed; some early residents, such as the Peter family, connected on the highest levels, but there was also a glass manufactory and lime kilns. The British ambassador resided on a hill above Pennsylvania Avenue, and the earliest federal offices occupied portions of the "Six Buildings" on the avenue itself. The U.S. Naval Observatory, a major federal (and scientific) institution, capped the heights of Camp Hill. To the east lay the cottage of David Burnes, one of the neighborhood's earliest homes, soon joined by a splendid mansion built by his son-in-law. Immediately south of the cottage lay the path of the canal linking the City Canal along what is now the National Mall to the Chesapeake and Ohio Canal, debouching into Rock Creek. A landmark along the canal was Braddock's Rock, where General Braddock and George Washington landed in 1755 en route to defeat at Fort Duquesne in the French and Indian War.

Uphill from the Burnes Cottage and Van Ness Mansion at the corner of New York Avenue and Eighteenth Street lay the Octagon House, built at the close of the eighteenth century. It would serve as a temporary lodging for the President and Mrs. Madison following the burning of the White House in 1814. Federal executive offices clustered close to the White House began to spread into Foggy Bottom—the first being the Winder Building in 1848. The Civil War led to an increased Federal presence, including the military encampment known as Camp Fry, which was built south of Washington Circle. The most prominent landmark in the area, Washington Circle, was "the Circle" for many years, with the Clark Mills' equestrian statue of President Washington, dedicated in 1860, at its center.

After the Civil War, Foggy Bottom and the West End entered a new stage of growth. Modest brick houses began to fill the empty spaces at the center of the area. Blocks that would later be decried as slums occupied the northern, western and southern fringes. New industries came, including several breweries—those of Abner-Drury and Christian Heurich being the most famous. Churches (Episcopal, Catholic, Baptist, Lutheran, Methodist and others), which had already been in operation, built new, expanded edifices to meet the demands of the increasing population. To the east, near the White House, prominent citizens clustered in homes newer than those around Lafayette Square but slightly more modest than those rising at Pacific (later Dupont) Circle.

As the century turned, nearby engineering feats helped transform the area. The canal bed in Foggy Bottom was replaced by an extended B Street, renamed Constitution Avenue. The mud flats in the Potomac River, exacerbated by Long Bridge, were reclaimed and transformed into East and West Potomac Park. The 1902 McMillan Commission proposals brought the new parkland into a grandly extended Mall, terminated with a grand monument (initially slated to be for Grant but later changed to honor Lincoln). There would also be a new monumental bridge crossing the Potomac to Arlington.

Removal of the mud flats and canal improved the health of the area, which had been unsanitary—inhabitants of the observatory had been afflicted with yellow fever borne by mosquitoes. But despite the improvement in conditions, the observatory decamped for higher altitudes several miles to the north.

In a development that was innocuous at the time, George Washington University, the recently renamed Columbian University, moved to the area in 1912. The blocks in which it located were home to a select portion of Washington's elite. It was here that the university grew and flourished, eventually helping displace that elite, as well as other residents.

A variety of redevelopment efforts converged on Foggy Bottom and the West End as the twentieth century progressed. Private development, exemplified by Potomac Plaza at Virginia and New Hampshire Avenues, occurred even as planners decreed that only comprehensive federal efforts would suffice. A thirty-eight-block proposal to redevelop virtually the entire neighborhood was eventually defeated, and a much-reduced development was created instead: the mixed-use Columbia Plaza complex. Some nearby alley dwellings were displaced by the St. Mary's apartment for seniors, but others were saved. The entire West End also underwent a series of planning exercises; it would eventually transform from a mix of car dealerships and small commercial enterprises into an extension of downtown with a smattering of high-rise residential buildings.

Historic preservation efforts are also well represented in Foggy Bottom. A small historic district was created in 1987, comprising almost 150 residential structures in four city blocks. These represent the "modest, working-class" character of some housing in the neighborhood. The Octagon and Red Lion Row were preserved, albeit with large office buildings looming behind.

INTRODUCTION

Federal buildings came in great numbers in the twentieth century: the General Services Administration in 1917, the Department of the Interior in 1918 and the War Department in 1941. The latter was declared too small to meet the demands of a country at war, and the building was given over to the State Department. Constitution Avenue became the address for monumental buildings to house the Pan-American Union (now the Organization of American States), the Federal Reserve and the American Institute of Pharmacy. The Red Cross took a block on E Street and later expanded. The World Bank and International Monetary Fund both decided to locate in the area and then expand. Culture came to Foggy Bottom in a big way with the construction of the John F. Kennedy Center for the Performing Arts, which displaced portions of the old Riverside Stadium and Heurich Brewery. The Pan-American Health Organization was built north of the State Department building, next to the local fragment of the grand interstate freeway system planned (but only partially completed) to bisect central Washington. Along the Potomac, the gasworks was torn down to make way for the Watergate complex, locally famous for its prestigious inhabitants and nationally infamous as the site of the break-in at the Democratic National Party Headquarters in 1972.

Now, Foggy Bottom and the West End have entered the twenty-first century, and they continue to reflect changes in the larger city around them. Columbia Hospital has become upscale condos, and a new Peace Institute has risen at the foot of Camp Hill, directly across a highway onramp from the small boulder that is the remnant of Braddock's Rock. It has always been this way in these neighborhoods sandwiched between the White House and Georgetown. As the city has changed, so have they. In this small corner of Washington, local and federal, residential and commercial, small and grand, have all bumped up against one another. The following photographs and other illustrations show these various forces at work—creating history even as they replace the history that came before.

EARLY HISTORY

In 1765, Jacob Funk laid out Hamburgh in what was then Maryland, just downriver from the fall-line town of Georgetown. It encompassed some hilly land sloping to the waterfront, just east of the mouth of Goose (Tiber) Creek. Little development had taken place, however, before a dramatic development occurred: President George Washington proposed moving the nation's capital to the vicinity of Funk's holdings. Discussion ensued over the appropriate size of the new city, with Thomas Jefferson proposing a modest, several-block area centered on Hamburgh. The ultimate plan of L'Enfant and Washington spanned the entire plain from the Potomac to the Eastern Branch. The Hamburgh/Foggy Bottom area did not become the capital but would sit just west of the new presidential palace.

This fortuitous siting drove much of the development of Foggy Bottom. The origin of the name is lost in the mists of history, so to speak, but one might imagine a vapor rising from the marshy area around Goose Creek immediately below the low outcropping that would come to be known as Camp Hill. The designation may have been necessary to distinguish the area from "Round Tops," north of Pennsylvania Avenue and Washington Circle, which was in turn named not after geography but after the architecture of several early homes that were topped with cupolas. The exact extent of the Foggy Bottom neighborhood is also debated. "Deep" Foggy Bottom extends from Twenty-third Street to the Potomac, but the neighborhood generally can be considered to run from Seventeenth Street to the Potomac and north to Pennsylvania Avenue, with the West End (a 1970s designation) stretching up to N Street and east to New Hampshire Avenue. For many years, the entire area was known as the First Ward.

The First Ward developed south from a core along the Pennsylvania Avenue thoroughfare to Georgetown and west from Seventeenth Street as homes and government buildings were built. Most of the early development (or at least that which survived long enough to warrant being photographed) was for the wealthy, and the first settlers had prominent connections. The Peter family, for instance, which occupied homes on K Street near Georgetown, was related by marriage to President Washington himself. Substantial homes joined those of the Peters on Pennsylvania Avenue. One of them housed the British ambassador. Another prominent family, the Tayloes, chose to build closer to the White House on New York Avenue, from whence they enjoyed a splendid view of the Potomac River. Near the river itself was the Van Ness Mansion. The western edge of the neighborhood was initially developed more densely, following the pattern set in Georgetown. Homes on the eastern edge, while certainly stately and cosmopolitan, tended to leave space between them, such as in the case of the Octagon House or the Van Ness Mansion.

Development also occurred along the waterfront in the vicinity of William Easby's wharf. Wilhelmine Easby Smith (daughter of shipyard owner Easby) would describe in 1913 the changes that had occurred in the area since her childhood:

> Lately I visited the old home of my childhood, but the place was well nigh unrecognizable. The dwelling house, large for those days, is transformed into a blacksmith's shop, and the upper rooms into a depository for junk.
>
> The old garden, which occupied nearly half the square except the corner lot where dwelt the Ferguson family, has disappeared. The luscious fruit—figs, grapes, apples, pears, prunes, and rare flowers that attracted many visitors, have long since perished. This part of the property is now covered by the buildings of Littlefield and Alvord.
>
> The bridge that spanned the canal is gone, for the canal is no longer there. The bells of the mules have ceased to jingle, their drivers' calls are hushed.

Despite the cluster of buildings around the wharf, much of the southern stretches of Foggy Bottom remained relatively barren, even after the observatory was established nearby on Camp Hill at Twenty-third and E Streets.

Early History

The Civil War brought many changes to Washington. In Foggy Bottom, the construction of Camp Fry, just south of Washington Circle on both sides of Twenty-third Street, spurred development of the center of the neighborhood. Camp Fry was the home to the Invalid Corps (renamed the Veteran Reserve Corps in 1864)—invalid soldiers stationed to guard public properties throughout Washington City and serve in the defenses of Washington. As one ditty ("Invalid Corps" by Frank Wilder, 1863) would have it:

> *I wanted much to go to war,*
> *And went to be examined;*
> *The surgeon looked me o'er and o'er,*
> *My back and chest he hammered.*
> *Said he, You're not the man for me,*
> *Your lungs are much affected,*
> *And likewise both your eyes are cock'd,*
> *And otherwise defected.*
>
> *[Chorus]*
> *So, now I'm with the invalids,*
> *And cannot go and fight, sir!*
> *The doctor told me so, you know,*
> *Of course it must be right, sir!*

After the Civil War, the pace of growth in Foggy Bottom and the West End slowed. Most development remained focused on the area above F Street. The completion of the Washington Monument at the southeast corner of the neighborhood gave photographers a vantage point from which to record the area's growth, or lack thereof. Reopening the Washington branch of the Chesapeake and Ohio Canal, disused since the 1850s, was discussed, and this likely could have brought more rapid growth to Foggy Bottom. But the canal soon was filled in, leaving only the lock keeper's house as evidence of its existence.

Braddock Rock, pictured here, is the remnant of a much larger rocky outcrop where (traditionally, but doubtfully), in 1755, British General Braddock, accompanied by young Lieutenant Colonel George Washington, landed his troops en route to ultimate defeat at Fort Duquesne. The Rock (sometimes called the "Key of all Keys") served as a survey marker in early city development. Now hidden at the bottom of a well shaft, the Rock has been whittled away, quarried for various private and public buildings (including reputedly the White House and Capitol). Much of the Rock was blasted away in the 1830s for the eastward extension of the Chesapeake and Ohio Canal to the Washington Canal. *(LC)*

Before this section of Maryland was designated part of the nation's capital, a number of towns sprang up along the Potomac and its Eastern Branch—Georgetown at the fall line of the Potomac and Bladensburg up the Eastern Branch. Two more towns were laid out but never developed (so-called paper towns)—Carrollsburg at the mouth of the Eastern Branch and Hamburgh where Goose (Tiber) Creek met the Potomac. The latter was laid out on 220 acres in 1765 by a German immigrant named Jacob Funk. The house shown in this 1930s photo was one of the few built in Hamburgh and dates from circa 1790. *(LC)*

This measured drawing of the Hamburgh house at what would become 412 Twentieth Street NW shows a simple, handsome structure documented before its destruction in March 1935. *(LC)*

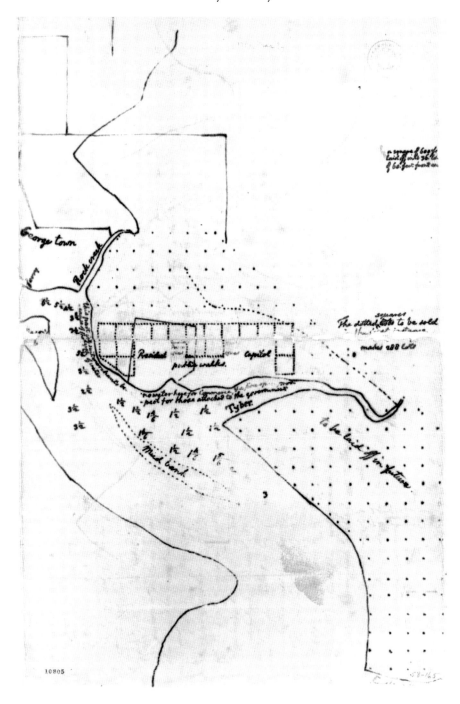

This 1791 sketch by Thomas Jefferson offers his idea of how the capital might be laid out. His modest plan extended little beyond today's downtown, placing the Capitol where today's White House is and a house for the president sited in mid-Foggy Bottom. *(LC)*

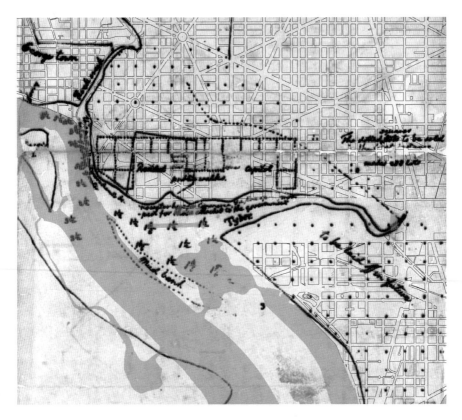

Here, superimposed on today's Washington streetscape, Jefferson's sketch shows the relation of Jacob Funk's Hamburgh, Jefferson's own proposed city plan and today's heritage of the adopted L'Enfant plan. *Courtesy Matthew Gilmore.*

To the east of Hamburgh, near today's Seventeenth Street and Constitution Avenue, was David Burnes's home (or cottage). Burnes, one of the original proprietors (landowners) in the new capital (and evidently a hard bargainer), was described by George Washington as "that obstinate man." Washington may have been speaking in jest. The cottage would survive as a romantic ruin up to the start of the twentieth century. *(DCPL)*

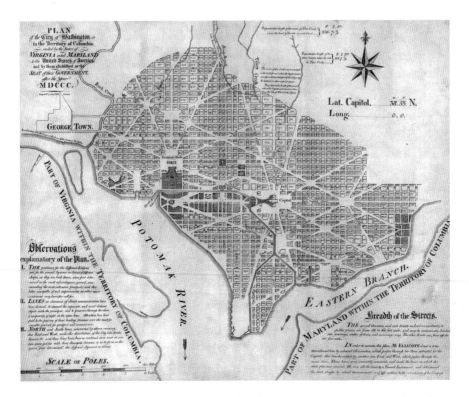

The L'Enfant plan (or perhaps more properly, L'Enfant-Ellicott plan) was the creation of Peter Charles L'Enfant under commission of George Washington, who intended a grand design for the new capital. Unlike Jefferson's sketch, the plan encompassed many square miles, spanning the plain from Georgetown to the Eastern Branch of the Potomac. After L'Enfant's dismissal, Andrew Ellicott made relatively minor changes to the plan. The new plan displaced Hamburgh and Carrollsburg. *(LC)*

David Burnes's daughter, Marcia, inheritrix of her father's substantial real estate holdings, was the wealthiest woman in the new capital. In 1802, she married John P. Van Ness. She died in 1832. *(LC)*

John P. Van Ness, congressman from New York, married Marcia Burnes and became a fixture in the Washington social scene for the next forty years. He was mayor from 1830 to 1834. *(LC)*

The Van Nesses built an elegant home to the east of the Burnes Cottage, completed in 1820 and long a local landmark. *(LC)*

Before they were demolished to make way for the Inner Loop Freeway, the Peter Houses at 2618 and 2620 K Street NW bore a plaque placed there by the Daughters of the American Revolution that stated, "George Washington was a guest in this house on his last night in this city, August 5, 1799. David Erskine, British minister and friend of America, occupied it 1806–1809." The first house in the group was built circa 1794 by Robert Peter for his son, Thomas Peter, and his wife, Martha Parke Custis, a step-niece of the later famous guest. *(DCPL)*

Nearer to the White House, the Tayloe family built, in 1800, a home that would come to be known as the Octagon. Prominently located at the corner of Eighteenth Street and New York Avenue and designed by William Thornton, it is not actually eight-sided. Here the Madisons took shelter after the British burned the White House in the War of 1812, and here the Treaty of Ghent ending the war was signed. The Tayloe family lived in the house until 1855. The house then saw a sad decline, ultimately serving as a boardinghouse until it was purchased by the American Institute of Architects in 1899 to serve as the institute's headquarters. It was landmarked in 1961 and opened as a museum in 1970. *(LC)*

The Octagon had extensive grounds and outbuildings, some indication of which can be seen in this view of the estate in 1913. *(LC)*

Opposite, bottom: This is the Historic American Buildings Survey's reconstruction of the original Easby Home. *(LC)*

Early History

The Easby Home just east of the Observatory was built in the 1830s, adjacent to William Easby's wharf. *(LC)*

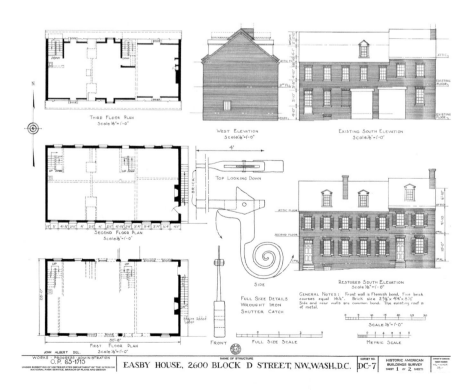

Another early notable home was that of Mayor Thomas Carbery, located at Seventeenth and C Streets. It would be known as "Miracle House" for the miraculous healing of the mayor's sister, Ann Carbery Mattingly, in 1824. This image shows the house shortly before its demolition in 1903. This is now the site of the Daughters of the American Revolution Memorial Continental Hall. *(LC)*

Number 2411 Pennsylvania Avenue was part of the first wave of construction in Foggy Bottom and the West End, having been built in the early 1800s. This photo is from 1936, shortly before its demolition. The house served as the British legation during the Jefferson administration. Perhaps Irish poet Thomas Moore wrote "Last Rose of Summer" here, but more likely he penned the following satirical lines: "Come, let me lead thee o'er this 'second Rome! / ... / what was Goose-Creek once is Tiber now: / This embryo capital, where Fancy sees / Squares in morasses, obelisks in trees; / Which second-sighted seers, even now, adorn / With shrines unbuilt and heroes yet unborn, / Though naught but woods and Jefferson they see, / Where streets should run and sages *ought* to be." *(LC)*

The 2100 block of Pennsylvania Avenue was known as the "Six Buildings" (the end building was added later). Built in the 1790s, the State and Navy Departments made their home here in 1800, when the government moved to the new capital. *(DCPL)*

The earliest photograph of the U.S. Naval Observatory. The observatory for a time marked the national meridian. Astronomer Asaph Hall discovered the moons of Mars through its main telescope. Built in the 1840s, the observatory served its national purpose and a local one, marking noon each day with the dropping of a ball on its flagstaff, allowing Washingtonians to accurately set their watches. In 1894, the observatory decamped to higher grounds, and the U.S. Naval Hospital was located here. *(LC)*

Number 2300 K Street, St. Ann's Infant Asylum. From 1867 and for the next eighty-three years, St. Ann's occupied this building, once the British legation, and became identified with the following phrase: "When there was nowhere else to turn, St. Ann's was there." The building was razed in 1948. *(DCPL)*

The Pennsylvania Avenue Bridge across Rock Creek, connecting Georgetown to Foggy Bottom and the rest of the city. The innovative arched cast-iron pipes carry water from the Washington Aqueduct. The bridge was engineered by Montgomery Meigs and completed in 1860; it would be named after Meigs in 1862. The bridge was encased in concrete in 1915–16 (and again named after Meigs), prompting debate in the government design community over the proper design of Rock Creek bridges. *(DCPL)*

A pastoral image of Foggy Bottom looking toward the Georgetown waterfront in 1855. The observer would have had the observatory at his back. One of the structures along the river in this image could be the Easby Home. *(LC)*

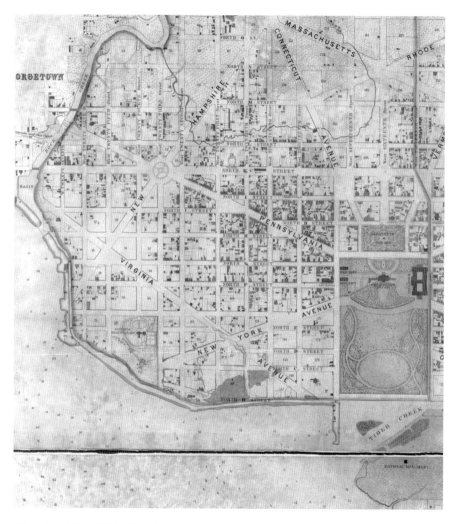

Albert Boschke published in 1856 an impressive map of Washington City. This detail of Foggy Bottom shows the existing buildings and the route of the canal. *(LC)*

The canal lock keeper's house at Seventeenth and B Streets (now Constitution Avenue) was built about 1835. The house is the last remnant of the Washington Branch of the Chesapeake and Ohio Canal. This branch skirted Foggy Bottom along the Potomac shore and linked Georgetown to the Washington City Canal south of the White House. The canal fell into disrepair in the 1850s and was abandoned. The house was used as a residence—Elizabeth Kytle, in her memoir, reports that her grandmother lived in the house before the Civil War. Later, it was the U.S. Park Police headquarters. *(DCPL)*

General Grant's headquarters at Seventeenth and F Streets in a contemporary engraving. The building was erected by Colonel Nathan Towson, paymaster general of the armies, in 1819 and was used by General Winfield Scott until his retirement. *(DCPL)*

Here is General Grant's headquarters years later with a third story added, now with the address of 532 Seventeenth Street. The building would be the home of the National Council for the Prevention of War in the 1920s and 1930s. Despite its historic associations, it was demolished for a parking lot in 1947. The site today is the headquarters of the Federal Deposit Insurance Commission. *(LC)*

The Winder Building at Seventeenth and F Streets served as the Civil War headquarters for various military offices and had the Central Signal Station, shown here, on its roof. A number of myths surround the building—commanding generals were not headquartered here, nor did Lincoln visit to read telegraphic dispatches or visit prisoners of war. William H. Winder erected the building in 1848 to lease to the federal government, probably commissioning Robert Mills as the designer. *(LC)*

Camp Fry, viewed from Washington Circle. Camp Fry was home to the Ninth and Tenth Veteran Reserve Corps, originally dubbed the "Invalid Corps." These troops had been invalided out of active service and were stationed as guards around various federal buildings in the city. *(LC)*

A picture of Veteran Reserve Corps members taken on April 10, 1865, the day after General Lee's surrender. Here musical instruments take center stage, with the band of the Ninth Veteran Reserve Corps in dress uniform. Note the young lady and girls at the far right, the soldiers in the background and the bandstand (as well as the statue of George Washington). *(LC)*

Company B, Tenth Veteran Reserve Corps. Here the young ladies have collected their hoops; the fence around Washington Circle is more clearly visible, as is a soldier in the bandstand. *(LC)*

The girls have their hoops, and a little boy has joined the scene, as has an observer in the trees behind. This photo shows the noncommissioned officers of Company H, Tenth Veteran Reserve Corps. *(LC)*

Company I, Ninth Veteran Reserve Corps. *(LC)*

Here the band is in the bandstand. Note the tiny drummer boy on the far left. This is Company C, Tenth Veteran Reserve Corps. *(LC)*

Company F, Veteran Reserve Corps. *(LC)*

The northernmost buildings of Camp Fry are visible where they meet Washington Circle. Pictured is Company C, Tenth Veteran Reserve Corps. *(LC)*

Foggy Bottom detail of the 1884 Adolph Sachse print of Washington, D.C. Sachse's is a lightly idealized early springtime landscape, sprinkled with trees. Missing are a few important features, such as the gas tanks. *(LC)*

This 1885 photograph shows Foggy Bottom looking northwest along Virginia Avenue toward Georgetown. The canal had skirted Foggy Bottom on the south and west, along a path here marked with trees. Excavation can be seen along Virginia Avenue, between Nineteenth and Twentieth—probably for sewerage. *(DCPL)*

Another elevated view, circa 1903, shows Virginia Avenue and H Street from atop the largest gas tank in Foggy Bottom, looking toward the smoky industrial Georgetown waterfront. The ship docked at the waterfront would have been delivering coal for gasification. *(DCPL)*

The view from Twenty-fifth and E Streets in 1913. This shows a more rural, picturesque landscape. *(LC)*

AT WORK

Foggy Bottom and the West End were for many years a mix of all kinds of land uses, from residential to industrial, a contrast to expectations for a city with a reputation for having only one business—politics. Industry came early to the area with enterprises like the Glass House factory on the waterfront, William Easby's shipyard and the Godey limekilns, among others.

George and Andrew Way started their glass factory in 1807, and there would be workers making glass near where Twenty-second Street ended at the river until the 1850s. The complex was large for the time, consisting of a blowing room, a flattening house, a cutting room, a pot room, a mixing room, a box shop and a wood yard used to fuel the works. Nearby was William Easby's shipyard. Easby had worked at the Washington Navy Yard, leaving in 1825 to start his own business. It was a success and produced revenue cutters for the U.S. Coast Guard—ships designed to enforce trade restrictions and prevent smuggling. Slightly to the west, the Godey limekilns at the mouth of Rock Creek derive their name from William H. Godey, who operated them in the second half of the nineteenth century. Limestone was brought by canalboat from Seneca, Maryland. It was then heated to produce lime, which was used in the mortar utilized to construct much of red-brick Washington.

After these early industrial adventures, two industries, more than any others, eventually came to signify Foggy Bottom—gas and brewing. Gas tanks were first built on Virginia and New Hampshire Avenues in 1856. The gasworks turned coal into gas for heating, cooking and lighting. It grew for almost a century, adding more tanks to serve the growing demands of the city. The plant and its associated tanks were not demolished until 1948.

Brewing became one of the area's signature industries with the construction of the fantastic brick castle of the Heurich Brewery in the 1890s. Heurich's previous brewery to the north had burned down, leading to his determination to build securely in brick. Of the brewery's thirteen labels, Senate, Heurich and Old Georgetown were the most popular. The brewery survived Prohibition by making and selling ice, including amongst its clients the U.S. Congress and the Supreme Court. Beer brewing returned after the end of Prohibition, but the national distribution of competing brands led to the decision to close the brewery in 1956. Christian Heurich died in 1945 at age 102, and the brewing complex was demolished in 1961. In addition to the Heurich Brewery, the Abner-Drury Brewery was another major employer.

Also sprinkled throughout both Foggy Bottom and the West End were heavy and light industries—ironworks, such as Gichner and several others; Cranford Paving Company; cleaners; lithographers; a dairy; and publishers. The Gichner factory's first business was creating decorative ironwork, but after World War II it switched to building trucks for the navy. A.F. Jorss ironworks was located next door in the West End and also had its start manufacturing decorative ironwork. Cranford Paving Company occupied the area of the Potomac waterfront that had been Easby's wharf. Cranford was noted for many advances in the paving and concrete business. The company was founded in 1872, and by the time of the 1940 death of Joseph Cranford, son of the founder, it had laid over one million square yards of pavement. In a related twentieth-century development, garages and automobile dealers would make their home in the West End, the best-known being Washington Packard, later Capital Cadillac. The West End maintained its small factories and automobile shops longer than Foggy Bottom because there were fewer institutional pressures.

Pennsylvania Avenue served as the main neighborhood commercial strip. Early in the area's history, a typical urban mix of commercial establishments filled the Six Buildings and Seven Buildings on the north side of the avenue and what would later be called Red Lion Row on the south side. Off the avenue, a notable commercial fixture for years was Marjorie Hendricks's Water Gate Inn. Hendricks had converted a former riding school at Twenty-seventh and F Streets in 1942 into a homey restaurant offering up Pennsylvania Dutch food. Another notable restaurant was Blackie's House of Beef, located in the West End. Ulysses "Blackie" Auger began in the food service business in 1946, running a noontime hotdog stand at Twenty-second and M Streets. He then opened a restaurant called the Minute Grille. Financial assistance from neighbor (and proprietor of Capital Cadillac) Floyd Akers helped him open a new spot when that lease expired.

Blackie's catered to office-bound businessmen and would thus last longer than Capital Cadillac, but both would eventually be displaced. The average Foggy Bottom or West End employee would go from making things in a factory or tinkering under the hood of a car to working behind a computer at a desk.

Shown here from the Potomac in an 1839 engraving by Augustus Koellner, the Glass House was one of the first major industries in Foggy Bottom. In the early years of its operation, the glass factory advertised that it would ship its main product—window glass—anywhere on the continent. *(LC)*

This view from the Georgetown end of the Chesapeake and Ohio Canal, looking toward Foggy Bottom, shows the Godey limekilns in the distance on the right. *(LC)*

This is a closer view of the ruins of the limekilns. *(LC)*

Gas tanks at Virginia and New Hampshire Avenues. The first tank was built as early as 1856. Washington Gas Light was a major presence and employer in the area for many years. Streetcar tracks appear at the near edge of this photograph. *(LC)*

Another perspective on the same scene. Foggy Bottom's name may derive in part from, or at least may have been perpetuated as a result of, the presence of the gas manufacturing operation. When the plant was first built, some people erroneously thought that the gasification process might dispel the area's fogginess. *(LC)*

At Work

The Foggy Bottom and West End were home to a wide variety of commercial and industrial establishments. Here is a view of the Twenty-fourth and M Streets Garage in 1920, when war veteran "Brailey" Gish was manager. The garage had been taken over by the federal government for storage during World War I. It became Barrett Garage in 1921, but the Motor Company of Washington reserved a space for its line of Stutz and Auburn passenger vehicles. *(LC)*

Twenty-sixth Street and Pennsylvania Avenue was the location of Chestnut Farms Dairy. *(Star)*

This interior image shows the Chestnut Farms bottling equipment. Milk was a controversial subject in the postwar era and subject to heavy restrictions and price controls. *(LC)*

Here at Twenty-second and M Streets are the offices and printing plant of the *United States Daily*. The *Daily* was started by David Lawrence in 1926 as a sheet devoted to government news—absolutely nonpartisan and with no editorial content. It was succeeded by *United States News* in 1933, the precursor to today's *U.S. News and World Report*. This image was probably taken after the 1928 expansion of the plant. *(LC)*

Another major employer in Foggy Bottom was Cranford Paving Company. One of its major paving accomplishments is pictured here: Taft Bridge, which carries Connecticut Avenue over Rock Creek Park. *(LC)*

Heurich Brewery was a well-known business in the neighborhood. The first Heurich Brewery was at 1229 Twentieth Street on the edge of the West End. Christian Heurich built the new brewery in Foggy Bottom in 1894–95 at D and Twenty-fifth Streets. *(LC)*

Having lost his first brewery to fire, Heurich was determined not to suffer the same fate again and built a fantastic brick brewing complex. *(Star)*

Here is the Heurich bottling equipment. There was one major brewing competitor to Heurich in the neighborhood at Twenty-fifth and G Streets: the Abner-Drury Brewery, organized in 1898 and closed in 1938. *(Star)*

Another long-lived local business was Congers laundry, located at the corner of New York Avenue and Twenty-third and C Streets, where now a new annex to the American Pharmacists Association building has just been constructed in 2009. This is a view along C Street toward Twenty-third. C.C. Conger founded the business in 1903. *(HSW)*

On the opposite end of Foggy Bottom, adjacent to the White House, service and financial industries proliferated. Here is the 1923 architectural rendering of Washington Loan and Trust's branch at Seventeenth and G Streets. The "West End" branch was designed (ostensibly) to conform to adjacent federal buildings. Noted architect Arthur B. Heaton was the designer. *(LC)*

Pennsylvania Avenue hosted a wide variety of businesses. This photo from 1921 shows automobile supplies, groceries and a drugstore standing side by side in the 1900 block, just west of the storied Seven Buildings. Contemporary newspapers encouraged the proper care and maintenance of your Willard Storage Battery. *(LC)*

Marjorie Hendricks, proprietor of the Water Gate Inn, a can of her famous onion soup in hand. She also operated the Normandy Farm in Montgomery County, Maryland. *(Star)*

Hendricks's restaurant, opened in 1942, had rustic charm, punctuated by the signature hobbyhorse with authentic reproduction Dutch furniture. She specialized in solid Pennsylvania Dutch food and was famous for her trademark popovers. Water Gate Inn was demolished for the Kennedy Center. *(Star)*

Another noted neighborhood business owner was Floyd Akers, seen here receiving a Gib Crockett caricature as a reward for leading the community war fund. Akers owned Capital Cadillac. *(Star)*

Above: Ulysses "Augie" Blacker ran Blackie's House of Beef in the West End until quite recently, when it closed in 2006. *(Star)*

Right: An informal ambiance in Blackie's was conveyed by the checkered tablecloths and rustic wall decorations. *(Star)*

Even some of the littlest denizens of the neighborhood worked; these young newsboys lived in Foggy Bottom and worked in downtown, hawking newspapers. The original photo caption reads: "After midnight April 17, 1912 G St., near 14th, these three boys 10 yrs., 11 yrs. and 12 yrs. old, were stuck with over 50 papers on their hands, and vowed they would stay until they sold out if it took all night. The oldest said, 'my mother makes me sell.' Lawrence Lee (age 10) 912 26th Street NW, Michael Niland (age 11) 930 26th Street NW, Martin Garvin (age 12) 928 26th Street NW." *(LC)*

At Home

Substantial residential development in Foggy Bottom and the West End began after the Civil War. The growth extended some already established patterns. Fine residences followed the Octagon and Ringgold-Carroll House to cluster on the east end of Foggy Bottom near the White House. Worker housing was established in the lowlands close to the river and Rock Creek and would eventually extend northward, engulfing the scattered homes that had been built on the edge of Georgetown, like the Peter Houses. The worker housing would leapfrog over Pennsylvania Avenue into the West End, while the avenue itself remained a mixture of shops and middle-class row homes. In between the working-class housing on the west and the stately homes on the east, middle-class dwellings would extend outward from the L'Enfant reservation that became Washington Circle. Most of the band of ground between Virginia Avenue and Pennsylvania Avenue from Seventeenth Street to Rock Creek would be filled in with homes by the mid-1880s.

The *Elite List* of 1901 listed 151 noteworthy addresses in Foggy Bottom (including 36 residents of the Hotel Richmond at 528 Seventeenth Street). These homes were close not only to the seat of the executive branch at 1600 Pennsylvania Avenue but also to the numerous social clubs along H and I Streets. The neighborhood could boast prominent residents like Adolphus Greeley, explorer of the North Pole, and (briefly) Theodore Noyes, editor of the *Washington Star*.

The *Elite List* does not include a single address west of Twenty-third Street, though. That area attracted another sort of attention. In 1906, Charles Weller published a booklet called *Neglected Neighbors: In the Alleys, Shacks and*

Tenements of the National Capital. He would expand this into a 342-page book in 1909. Weller paid particular attention to some of the alleys in Foggy Bottom, like Hughes' Alley (also spelled "Hewes," between Twenty-fifth and Twenty-sixth, K and I Streets) and Snow's Court (one block to the east of Hughes'), which he thought led to "the hiding away of little communities which are thus encouraged to develop their own low standards of life without much interference from the general community."

Some of the worst housing was in the West End. In various government positions, including, ultimately, governor of the District of Columbia, Alexander Shepherd extended paved streets through Foggy Bottom in the 1870s, but the area north of M Street and south of D Street remained unpaved. Even the unpaved streets were regraded, though, and this left some homes in the neighborhood isolated on high islands or in holes compared to the height of the thoroughfare. The results were scenes of dilapidation almost rural in character, mixed closely with some of the city's few urban tenements.

The population of working-class Foggy Bottom was largely of German and Irish extraction during the Victorian era, with the Germans tending to be employed by the breweries and the Irish by the gasworks. This began to change in the 1920s as African Americans moved into the neighborhood, leading to a rapid demographic shift. As an example, the eighteenth-century Peter Houses were divided into apartments in 1900; all of them were rented to whites at that time. By 1910, there was one African American renter. By 1920, all of the tenants at the Peter Houses were African American.

The 1920s also saw an increase in the construction of apartment buildings. The federal government was expanding rapidly and bringing more clerks and bureaucrats to the city by the day. Three-story red brick Victorian Washington was not capable of meeting the increased housing demand, and the solution was to build taller and more compact buildings. High-rise apartments would continue to rise at an impressive speed well into the 1960s. The earliest multifamily buildings, like the Maury Apartments at Nineteenth and G Streets, were relatively modest in scale. These would give way to more ambitious structures, like the eight-story Mayfair and Potomac Park Apartments, and this general bulk would be maintained by all of the modern-style apartments built after World War II. The latter would wipe out much of the worker housing from the previous century, although this part of Foggy Bottom's legacy is still largely preserved between Twenty-fourth and Twenty-sixth, H and K Streets. Meanwhile, many of the earliest apartment buildings were later converted into dormitories or other uses for students at George Washington University, including the Everglades, the Flagler, the Keystone, Milton Hall and Munson Hall.

The southwest corner of Eighteenth and G Streets in 1903 was typical of the residential development on the eastern edge of Foggy Bottom. A variety of styles, from Federal to Victorian, line the street. The corner house, 622 Eighteenth Street, has been converted into a Young Ladies' Seminary. In 1937, Delos Smith of the Historic American Buildings Survey (HABS) would describe the structure as an "interesting brick corner house with unusually large window area." *(DCPL)*

Number 1744 G Street (also called the Edward Everett House) was opposite the Young Ladies' Seminary in the previous picture. It served various government functions after ceasing to be a private residence, including housing the Signal Service weather observation staff and the Naval Museum of Hygiene. Both corners are now occupied by modern office buildings, although in the block to the south the Victorian façades of Michler Row have been preserved. *(DCPL)*

Adolphus Washington Greely is an example of the class of gentlemen who lived in the blocks east of Twenty-third Street at the end of the nineteenth century, in this case at 1914 G Street. Greely was a famous polar explorer and career military officer. *(LC)*

Theodore Noyes attended the Columbian College (which later became George Washington University) before it relocated to Foggy Bottom. He moved to the Dakota Territory after his graduation. He returned in 1887 to Washington and briefly lived in Foggy Bottom at 837 Twenty-second Street (a small row house, still standing). Noyes maintained his links to the university, serving as a member of the board of trustees for over fifty years. *(LC)*

Woodhull House at 2033 G Street was built in 1855 in the Italianate style by Maxwell
Woodhull. It served as a private residence until his son donated the house to George
Washington University in 1921. *(LC)*

Another early house that helped establish the elite character of the neighborhood was the Ringgold-Carroll House at 1801 F Street (also called the John Marshall House after the chief justice who boarded there), built by Tench Ringgold in 1825. Today, it is the DACOR (Diplomatic and Consular Officers Retired) Bacon House and also houses the Ringgold-Marshall Museum. *(LC)*

Subsequent owners attempted to keep the Federal-style Ringgold-Carroll House current with its newer neighbors, such as by the addition of this iron gas lamp and rails. *(LC)*

Mrs. B.L. O'Leary's house at 2009 F Street was typical of a middle-class dwelling in Foggy Bottom. At the time of this photograph (circa 1925), the home was accepting boarders. *(LC)*

Left: This middle-class portion of Foggy Bottom on Twenty-third Street just south of Washington Circle was not long for the world when this photo was taken in 1947. These remaining two homes would be demolished to accommodate the George Washington University Hospital nearing completion behind them. *(DCPL)*

Below: Housing reformers particularly deplored living conditions in the alleys of Foggy Bottom, such as Snow's Court shown here. This was reportedly the first alley in Foggy Bottom with dwellings, the earliest dating back to the 1850s. *(DCPL)*

At Home

Sanitation was rudimentary in many poorer parts of Foggy Bottom and the West End in the late nineteenth century and early twentieth century. According to reformers, back lots and alleys were often awash in filth. This is part of an alley known as Rickett's (sometime Record or Rickard) Court, which was between Twenty-third, Twenty-fourth, E and F Streets, behind the Toner School, and was overlooked by the National Observatory on the hill immediately to the south. Rickett's was one of several Foggy Bottom alleys cited by Howard University professor William H. Jones in his *Recreation and Amusement Among Negroes in Washington, D.C.*, as having pathological child-raising conditions.

The dwellings of working-class Foggy Bottom, such as these from the now-demolished 2000 block of E Street, were generally flat-fronted and only ten to twelve feet wide. There were forty alley residences behind this row of homes. *(Star)*

Even modest dwellings featured some ornamental brickwork, such as the cornice in this row from the 2100 block of I Street. *(Star)*

West of Twenty-third Street and south of I Street, or north of Pennsylvania Avenue, homes mixed readily with industry, such as the gas tanks on Twenty-fifth Street near Virginia Avenue. *(DCPL)*

On the fringes of Foggy Bottom, a dilapidated wood-frame house could stand amongst overgrown lots. This photo shows Twenty-fifth Street (on the right), south of F Street in 1950. *(HSW)*

The growth of the federal government and the corresponding demand for housing in the early part of the twentieth century led to row homes being torn down and replaced by apartments. This is the Maury Apartments around 1921. Other apartment buildings in the block included the Akron, the Naples and the Monmouth. *(LC)*

Sometimes the rapidly expanding government took over the apartment buildings itself. Both the Mayfair (left) and Park Potomac (right) in the 2100 block of C Street had been appropriated for government offices by 1935. They would later be demolished to make way for the State Department. *(LC)*

By the early 1990s, modern apartment homes would become the dominant housing type for large sections of Foggy Bottom and the West End. Potomac Plaza, built on land purchased from the Washington Gas Light Company in 1952 and thus the first modern high-rise in the neighborhood, is the cruciform building in the center of this photograph. *(LC)*

ENTERTAINMENT

While Foggy Bottom and the West End were mostly residential and employment areas, they also housed places whose main purpose was to allow the citizens of the city to have fun.

Recreation was first provided for outdoors. For example, the landmark Van Ness Mansion fell into desuetude after General/Mayor Van Ness's death in 1846, and by the turn of the century, the grounds had been repurposed for a YMCA athletic park. Similarly, the reclamation of the Potomac flats and the creation of Potomac Park to the south, as well as the development of the parks along Virginia Avenue and Rawlins Park, led to increased chances for recreation, or at least a place to sit on a bench under a shade tree. Horseback riding in the parks was popular, and several riding schools settled along the Potomac shore, including the Potomac Riding Club and the Riverside Riding School. In 1924, there was a proposal that this form of recreation be extended to the masses with cheap government-controlled horses to explore Potomac and Rock Creek Parks.

In addition to outdoor recreation, large facilities were built to hold indoor events. Washington Auditorium opened in 1925 to fanfare as "Washington's Monument to Culture" and was reputedly the largest theatre of its kind, with seating for six thousand. Sited at the west end of Rawlins Park, the auditorium was one of the largest entertainment venues in the city. It featured a six-thousand-pipe Gibson-Moller pipe organ, showed movies and hosted such events as the annual auto show, but it was not a financial success. By the 1930s, Ernie Pyle would write a newspaper column describing the government workers' offices housed in the auditorium. The multipurpose auditorium was a precursor to today's Armory, Kennedy Center and Washington Convention Center. A more successful venue in Foggy Bottom would be George Washington University's Lisner Auditorium, which opened in 1943 and is still operating today at Twenty-first and H Streets.

Some venues straddled the line between outdoor and indoor. Riverside Stadium on the waterfront was originally built as an outdoor arena but was later enclosed. During its brief heyday in the 1940s, the stadium on the waterfront offered everything from ice-skating to football. It was the location for many local sports landmark events, including the D.C. Public Schools annual football championship, Georgetown University basketball, the Washington debut of the Ice Follies, the Washington Eagles hockey team and Joe Lewis's training camp in 1941. It had originally been built as an ice rink in 1938, and Severine Loeffler remodeled it as a roller-skating rink in 1942.

A few movie theatres were scattered around the neighborhood—the Mott (formerly Blue Mouse) on Twenty-sixth Street (serving primarily the African American population) and the Circle on Pennsylvania Avenue. Built in 1911, the Circle lasted into the 1980s. Penn Gardens, an enclosed theatre and open-air garden space, was built in 1914 on the hill at Twenty-first Street and Pennsylvania. After disputes with the police vice squad—charges including that of dancing too closely—the place reopened in 1921 as Jardin De St. Mark's. Dancing was allowed, although "strictly censored," but it would not last to the end of the Jazz Age and was replaced by an apartment building in 1928.

Live events, music and theatre found other homes in Foggy Bottom. Concerts by the National Symphony Orchestra took place five nights a week at the Watergate steps using a floating band shell—the audience was seated on the steps or floated in canoes alongside. A popular attraction beginning in 1935, the concerts ultimately fell victim, in the 1960s, to airplane noise from the nearby National Airport. Meanwhile, the Washington Theatre Club, founded by John and Hazel Wentworth, taught performance and produced plays beginning in the 1960s. Director Davey Marlin-Jones helped move the insurgent organization into the West End, into a former church, and into new activities, including jazz and an art gallery. The overextended organization folded in 1974.

The ultimate development in cultural facilities in the neighborhood would, of course, be the construction of the National Cultural Center (rechristened the John F. Kennedy Center for the Performing Arts before its opening) on the site of the Water Gate Inn. It became the home of the National Symphony Orchestra, as well as opera and theatre for the city and the region.

Above: The Van Ness Mansion went into steep decline after General Van Ness's death in 1846. By the early 1900s, its grounds were the YMCA Athletic Park. Note the broken windows (perhaps caused by a few foul balls) and the players' bicycles. *(DCPL)*

Right: A couple lounging at the YMCA Athletic Park under a tremendous oak. In the background is a big "All Welcome" sign. *(DCPL)*

The young lady, identified as Grace Williams, here pumps water from the antique water pump at the Van Ness Mansion in this photo from about 1904. *(DCPL)*

In the 1940s, the Riverside Stadium offered everything from skating to football. Rumor has it that it later also housed temporary offices for the CIA. *(HSW)*

In the 1920s, the short-lived Washington Auditorium briefly provided six thousand seats for performance-goers. After housing government offices, it was eventually demolished as part of the construction of the E Street Expressway. *(DCPL)*

Concerts were held at the Watergate, hosting the band on a floating concert shell on the river. Obviously a very popular draw, the concerts ultimately fell victim to noise from the nearby National Airport. *(LC)*

Here boaters and canoeists get perhaps the best seats in the house. *(DCPL)*

The Circle Theatre on Pennsylvania Avenue in the late 1940s. The theatre had been built in 1910 and was remodeled in 1935. It typifies the Art Deco architecture of Washington theatres but was demolished (despite being the oldest continuously operating theatre in Washington) for the construction of a massive office building for the International Monetary Fund. *(HSW)*

Hazel Wentworth was one of the driving forces behind the Washington Theatre Club. The club became one of Washington's premier live theatre venues. *(Star)*

The club's home, seen here, was at Twenty-third and L Streets, the former Union Wesley African Methodist Episcopal Church. The building served as the home of the Washington Theatre Club before transformation into the West End Cinema 1,2,3. *(Star)*

A Boy Scout event on D Street at Eighteenth in 1914, the site of Frazee Potomac Laundry. *(LC)*

Here the young men are seen in competition. *(LC)*

Rawlins Park served as a refuge for war workers, a green space amidst government buildings. *(LC)*

LOCAL INSTITUTIONS

Foggy Bottom and the West End have been home to numerous diverse institutions serving the people of the area and the city as a whole, from schools and charities to churches and hospitals.

Churches proliferated throughout the neighborhood. There were the Catholic St. Stephen's and the Episcopal St. Mary's, St. Paul's and St. Michael's. Presbyterians had Western Presbyterian Church. Baptists had Liberty, Mt. Lebanon and Gethsemane Baptist (both now relocated out of the neighborhood, displaced by the university) and the nearby Nineteenth Street Baptist Church. Union Wesley AME moved from Georgetown to the West End and then out of the area. Methodists and the United Church of Christ melded uniquely in the United Church (after failing to persuade Western Presbyterian to join as the third partner). No current Foggy Bottom congregation is in its original building, most having rebuilt or moved several times—either enhancing their sanctuary in situ or building anew after having been displaced by some larger institution.

Schools served the children of the neighborhood, both black and white—separately before *Bolling v. Sharpe* and together following that decision. These institutions included Analostan (Grant, now School Without Walls), Toner, Briggs, H.P. Montgomery, Weightman, Stevens and Francis Junior High. Grant/School without Walls and Francis are the only remaining and are still being used for classes. There were also private educational institutions, such as the Quaker Sidwell Friends (on Eighteenth Street until the 1930s) and St. Stephen's Catholic School at

Twenty-fourth and K Streets from 1924 to 1954 (replaced by Immaculate Conception Academy for Girls). Vocational education was represented by the renowned Lewis Hotel Training School located on Washington Circle.

Higher education came to Foggy Bottom in the 1910s. There was, of course, George Washington University but also others, such as American University. Columbian University originally was to occupy the Van Ness Mansion property, but that agreement (which gave the university its current name of George Washington University) fell through. The university instead occupied 2023 G Street (what had been St. Rose's Industrial School) and Woodhull House and has since grown to dominate central Foggy Bottom, which is a story quite unto itself.

Hospitals, current and past, anchored both sides of Foggy Bottom. Emergency Hospital was for years located on New York Avenue, and George Washington University Hospital would straddle one side or the other of Twenty-third Street from 1947 to the present day. In the West End, there was Columbia Hospital for Women in the 2400 block of L Street.

The Young Men's Christian Association had a long presence as a local institution. As noted in the "Entertainment" chapter, it used the former Van Ness estate as its athletic field. But it also built extensive facilities at Eighteenth and G Streets that included a reading room and gymnasium.

Charitable organizations of all kinds have been at home in Foggy Bottom and the West End, serving people in need from infancy to old age. These have included St. John's Orphanage, St. Rose's Industrial/Technical School for Girls, St. Ann's Infant Asylum, the House of Mercy, the Lenthall Home for Widows and Goodwill Industries. All are now gone or relocated. These local institutions, as well as many of the others shown in this chapter, largely gave way to the national and international institutions discussed in the following chapter.

St. Mary's Episcopal Church on Twenty-third Street. The church, built in the 1880s to serve the African American Episcopal community, was designed by noted architect James Renwick (who designed the Smithsonian). Nationalist and pan-Africanist Alexander Crummell presided over St. Mary's and then over its daughter church, St. Luke's. *(DCPL)*

Here the choir of St. Mary's poses on the church steps in 1900. *(DCPL)*

The interior of the old St. Paul's Episcopal Church on Twenty-third Street. The church dates back to 1866. In 1868, it became the first "free church" in Washington when it ceased the practice of renting pews. *(DCPL)*

Above: St. Paul's exterior. After a court battle, the land was condemned and the church was demolished for George Washington University Hospital, which was in turn demolished in 2006. St. Paul's relocated a few blocks away on K Street. *(DCPL)*

Left: St. Stephen's Catholic Church at Twenty-fifth Street and Pennsylvania Avenue, completed in 1868, was designed by Cluss and Kammerhueber. It was demolished in 1960 to make way for a new modern sanctuary. *(DCPL)*

Here the new church rises. *(DCPL)*

Union Methodist Church on Twentieth Street now houses media programs for George Washington University. Its first home on this site was built in 1846. The congregation merged with Concordia United Church of Christ to form the United Church in 1975. Western Presbyterian was to be the third partner in the union, but the congregation voted against the merger. *(DCPL)*

This church on Virginia Avenue served a succession of congregations—Holy Communion Chapel, then St. Michael's and All Angels Episcopal. In this image, it is Gethsemane Baptist. The site is now a George Washington University dormitory. *(HSW)*

Liberty Baptist's second sanctuary, on Twenty-third Street. Previously on E Street between Seventeenth and Eighteenth Streets, Liberty served the African American Baptist community. Church members are seen here leaving on a warm Sunday afternoon in the late 1940s. *(HSW)*

Union Wesley African Methodist Episcopal Church had its beginnings in 1848 in Georgetown but soon relocated to Twenty-third and L Streets due to racial persecution. This modern sanctuary built in 1948 was the last in a succession of buildings. *(HSW)*

The Friends Meetinghouse and School, located on I Street west of Eighteenth, served the Foggy Bottom neighborhood. The first meetinghouse was built in 1811, and a new building was constructed in 1879–80. A school was added in 1883—now the Sidwell Friends School located on Wisconsin Avenue in the Tenleytown neighborhood of Washington. *(SF)*

Here are primary school students on the steps of the Friends Meetinghouse in the 1930s. *(SF)*

The Friends school gymnasium in the 1910s. *(SF)*

The Weightman School in the 1940s. The school was one of many in the Foggy Bottom and West End neighborhoods. It was later used by various District government agencies and by the Selective Service during World War II. *(HSW)*

Briggs School at E and Twenty-second Streets, now long vanished due to the construction of the E Street Expressway in the early 1960s. *(Star)*

Above: Toner School at Twenty-fourth and F Streets, now part of the site of Columbia Plaza. *(Star)*

Left: Thaddeus Stevens School at Twenty-first and K Streets closed in 2008. Built in 1868, it was the first District school constructed with tax money for the education of African American children. *(Star)*

Cooking class at Francis Junior High School. Board of Education members inspect the proceedings. John R. Francis Junior High School, at Twenty-fifth and N Streets, was dedicated in 1928, built to serve the African American students of the neighborhood. *(Star)*

George Washington University at 2023 G Street. Formerly St. Rose's Technical School for Girls, this was the university's first home in Foggy Bottom, purchased in 1912. It was replaced by Lisner Library in 1939. *(LC)*

Stockton Hall at George Washington University. Part of a never-completed Georgian Revival quadrangle for George Washington University, it was built in 1924. *(LC)*

George Washington University students in the 1920s. *(LC)*

Foggy Bottom hosted multiple academic institutions besides George Washington University. Here at Nineteenth and F Streets is American University Graduate School, which opened in 1920. It is now the site of part of the World Bank. *(LC)*

Another neighborhood institution was the Young Men's Christian Association at Seventeenth and G Streets. Here young (and not so young) men make use of the library, bowler hats decorously doffed. *(LC)*

Above: The more athletically inclined could make use of the gymnasium, noted for its second level track. *(LC)*

Right: Many years later, George Washington University made use of the old YMCA to house students. There had been grander plans for expanding the Y, but it ultimately relocated to Seventeenth Street and Rhode Island Avenue. It was here that Walter Jenkins, an aide to President Johnson, was arrested in a sex scandal in 1964. *(Star)*

There were also several hospitals in the neighborhood; here is the first Columbia Hospital for Women, formerly the Maynard Mansion. The Rush-Bagot Treaty (which demilitarized the Great Lakes) was negotiated in this house, built by Tench Ringgold (who also built 1801 F Street). *(LC)*

The new Columbia Hospital, shown here under construction, was built in 1915. It was closed in 2002 and turned into condominiums. The monument to the Rush-Bagot Treaty, erected in 1935, is visible once again today. *(LC)*

Emergency Hospital was built in 1915 for $450,000. It was "one of the finest, if not the finest hospital in the world," according to contemporary newspaper accounts. The hospital was on New York Avenue between Seventeenth and Eighteenth Streets. *(LC)*

Emergency Hospital a few years later, before further expansions in the 1920s; a new wing designed by Appleton Clark was built in 1925. The tenth-floor solarium would have had one of the best views in the city, overlooking the White House and Washington Monument. *(LC)*

George Washington University Hospital (first building) under construction on the east side of Twenty-third Street, formerly the site of St. Paul's Episcopal Church. *(DCPL)*

Aerial view of the first GW Hospital and its neighborhood. The hospital, as well as the large apartment buildings, contrasts sharply with the row houses. The crisscross structures in the upper-right corner are temporary structures being used as university classrooms. St. Ann's can be seen to the west of Washington Circle. Streetcars are rounding the circle from both directions. *(DCPL)*

NATIONAL AND
INTERNATIONAL
INSTITUTIONS

Organizations of national and international importance have been located in Foggy Bottom and the West End almost since Washington became the capital. The chief of these are the various branches and offices of the federal government.

The first government offices in the neighborhood were the State and Navy Departments, which were housed in the Six Buildings on Pennsylvania Avenue. In the neighborhood's early history, war—both the actual act and the administration thereof—played an important role. The Octagon played host to the president and first lady after the burning of the White House during the War of 1812, and it was here that the treaty ending the war would be signed. Although less bellicose, the observatory was operated by the navy and was thus an important federal institution, as well as a neighborhood landmark, thanks to its position on Camp Hill. The Winder Building Annex to the War Department on the east end of Foggy Bottom would host various military offices, and during the Civil War, Camp Fry filled up the largely vacant area south of Washington Circle.

It was really in the twentieth century, though, that Foggy Bottom became indelibly linked with the federal government. Those blocks closest to the White House along Pennsylvania Avenue and Seventeenth Street accommodated a sprawl of federal offices. A glance at a contemporary 1920s map shows the Department of Labor, the Interstate Commerce Commission, the Civil Service Commission and the U.S. Navy west of Seventeenth Street on Pennsylvania and New York Avenues, F and G Streets. Farther away, the Weather Bureau made its long-term home in the West End, close to the Columbia Hospital for Women. During World War I, masses of temporary office buildings were thrown up, and these were only slowly replaced by permanent buildings for the Department of State, the Interior Department, the Federal Reserve and other agencies. Eventually, the whole of southern Foggy Bottom would be consumed by the federal government and a few institutional uses—so much so that planners termed it the "Federal Rectangle," corresponding to the Federal Triangle just east of the White House.

A new War Department building was proposed in 1936, deleted in 1937 and authorized by Congress in 1938, part of a very ambitious Public Works Administration program. The War Department was scattered through thirty buildings across the city at the time. The new building was sited across the street from the Interior Department at Twenty-first and D Streets. William Dewey Foster and Gilbert Stanley Underwood consulted on the design. John McShain, Inc., which would later build the Pentagon, handled the construction. It was designed in units, the first over 300,000 square feet. Ultimately, over 1 million square feet were planned, but events overtook the planning, and the War Department went to the Pentagon in Arlington rather than Foggy Bottom. The State Department took over the building that was meant for war, and "Foggy Bottom" would come to refer as much to this one agency as to the neighborhood itself.

Not all of the major institutions that located in Foggy Bottom were run by the government, however. Private or quasi-government organizations sought out the neighborhood just to be close to the center of the action. For instance, the Pan-American Union replaced the Van Ness Mansion and Burnes Cottage at Seventeenth Street and Constitution Avenue. A couple of hundred feet up Seventeenth Street, there was the headquarters of the Daughters of the American Revolution, the Corcoran Gallery of Art and the Red Cross. The World Bank and International Monetary Fund consumed real estate on Pennsylvania Avenue and nearby, displacing local institutions such as Western Presbyterian Church and the Circle Theatre. In the center of Foggy Bottom, the Pan-American Health Organization is located just north of the State Department on Twenty-third Street.

The neighborhood also became home to numerous monuments and memorials, beginning, of course, with the equestrian statue of George Washington in Washington Circle. Designed by Clark Mills and installed in 1860, it was the second equestrian statue in the city, the first being Mills's statue of Andrew Jackson in Lafayette Park. Washington Circle was the first of the city's circles to be landscaped and paved in 1856.

The *Titanic* memorial sculpted by Grace Vanderbilt Whitney was placed at the foot of E Street and New Hampshire Avenue and dedicated in 1931. It would later be moved to the southwest waterfront. In the 1950s and 1970s, a string of statues of Latin American revolutionary heroes were installed along Virginia Avenue, from the Pan-American Union to New Hampshire Avenue: José Artigas, Simon Bolivar, José de San Martín, Bernardo de Gálvez and Benito Juarez.

A piece of early Washington and American history: the treaty signing room in the Octagon. The plaque over the door reads, "The treaty of peace terminating the war of 1812 between the United States and Great Britain was signed in this room February 17, 1815." A replica of the treaty is in the glass case. *(LC)*

The statue of George Washington in Washington Circle. This circle, and others like it that were used to commemorate national heroes, extended the government presence out into the residential neighborhoods. *(LC)*

The Winder Building in a classic view—note the shabby condition of the exterior, the carriages and the two young men sitting in front of the building. The building was built by a private developer to house federal offices. This view dates from the 1870s, when extensive work was being done to plumb the city and regrade its streets. *(LC)*

The Weather Bureau at Twenty-fourth and M Streets was a fixture in the Foggy Bottom/ West End area for nearly one hundred years. The building was built in 1869 and redesigned by Alfred B. Mullett in 1884. It was demolished in 1965. *(NOAA)*

This is an image of the U.S. Food Administration Building under construction. A mixed African American and white work crew throw up one of a number of hastily constructed temporary buildings in the southern portion of Foggy Bottom. *(LC)*

This view shows the radical change that the First World War brought to Foggy Bottom. At least five massive temporary buildings fill the scene, all but crowding out the Pan-American Union, Daughters of the American Revolution and American Red Cross. The temporary buildings house the Fuel Administration, the Food Administration and a number of other agencies, as well as dormitories for war workers. The distant gas tanks and breweries of Foggy Bottom and the smokestacks of Georgetown are visible. In the immediate foreground is the lock keeper's house. *(LC)*

One of the temporary buildings, probably the Fuel Administration, years later. *(Star)*

The U.S. Fuel Administration maintained a library. *(LC)*

An interesting view of the entrance to the U.S. Fuel Administration. The wood and plaster construction has an almost medieval Tudor feel. *(LC)*

The lunchroom ladies of the Fuel Administration. *(LC)*

Despite the rudimentary construction of the building, the staff of the Fuel Administration seem well provisioned in their offices—personal typewriters, shared telephones. *(LC)*

The Fuel Administration is on the left, with the curious structure beyond being the U.S. Army quartermaster's garage. Far in the distance is the (Old) Post Office. Note the bales of hay on the truck. On the right is the War Trade Board building. *(LC)*

Here is the reverse view looking west: the Fuel Administration is at right, the War Trade Board at left. In the distance is one of the buildings of the U.S. Naval Medical School (housed in the old observatory). The differences shown here in the paving of C Street are quite amazing—beyond Twenty-first one can hardly tell there is a street. *(LC)*

"Temporary" buildings often persist far beyond expectations. In 1929, the Fuel Administration serves as a backdrop to this image of one of Secretary of War Stimson's goats. *(LC)*

Opposite, bottom: In this view a sparkling new Interior Building has displaced a number of temporary buildings, as well as the Frazee Potomac Laundry and the neighboring ironworks. D Street between Eighteenth and Nineteenth has also been closed. (LC)

One of the many signs from the U.S. Food Administration. Formed by executive order in 1917, the USFA was headed by "food dictator" Herbert Hoover, taking no salary. The administration encouraged self-sacrifice and had a pervasive and persuasive advertising campaign. *(LC)*

To the north is the venerable General Services Administration Building, separated from the Department of Interior Building by Rawlins Park. The statue of Rawlins, which had a peripatetic career before landing here, can be seen on the left, as can the Octagon on the right. *(DCPL)*

This photo provides just a glimpse of the elaborate decorations that went into the Interior Building, a stark contrast to the rough wood and plaster of the tempos. *(LC)*

One of the famous murals in the Department of the Interior Building: *The Negro's Contribution in the Social and Cultural Development of America*, by Millard Sheets. *(LC)*

This is one of the Interior Building's internal courtyards, not often seen by outsiders. *(LC)*

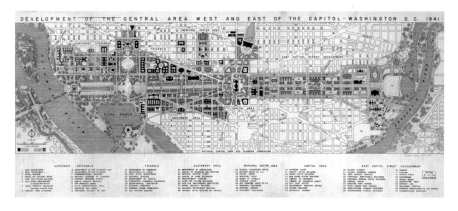

In 1941, the National Capital Planning Commission, planning for a postwar Washington, designated southern Foggy Bottom, with its heavy government presence, as the Federal or Northwest Rectangle. It suggested extending Rawlins Park westward and building a new naval museum, ship basin, Navy Department and extension to the War Department. This would complement the existing Federal Triangle to the east of the White House. *(LC)*

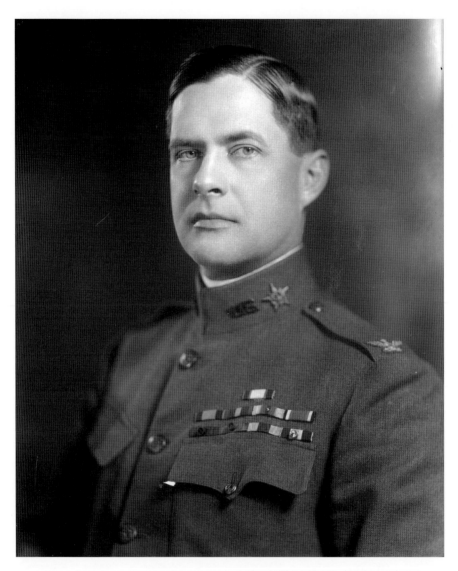

Ulysses S. Grant III was one of the leaders of change in Foggy Bottom, both in his role leading the National Capital Planning Commission and as the first vice-president of George Washington University. He would bring some of the architectural monumentalism of Constitution Avenue up Twenty-third Street with Tompkins Hall of Engineering. *(LC)*

This 1940 aerial view captures many of the changes in the area as the War Department is under construction. Most of the temporary offices are gone, but the quartermaster's garage (the large, almost round structure on Virginia Avenue) persists. Cars are parked seemingly everywhere. *(DCPL)*

When people refer to "Foggy Bottom," what they often mean is the U.S. State Department. The State Department moved into its building in the 1940s, and the War Department name (the original intended tenant) was chiseled off in 1947. The long-planned additional units (proposed in 1955) were completed in 1958, making State Building the largest office building in Washington at the time. McShain again was the construction contractor. The headquarters building was renamed after Harry S Truman in 2000. A George Marshall wing was added in 2001. *(Star)*

Right: A local institution meets a national one: in this photo from 1968, students in the "Career-In Resource Club" from Francis Junior High School make the trek eleven blocks south from school to visit the State Department. *(Star)*

Below: By the late nineteenth century, the Corcoran Art Gallery collection had outgrown its original red-brick building at Pennsylvania Avenue and Seventeenth Street. A new building was undertaken, with Ernest Flagg commissioned as architect. Ground was broken in 1893, and the gallery opened in 1897. *(LC)*

Here President Wilson and Chief Justice Taft lay the cornerstone for the American Red Cross building on Seventeenth Street, March 27, 1915. *(LC)*

Taft and Wilson at the ceremony. *(LC)*

The completed American Red Cross headquarters building. *(LC)*

National and International Institutions

Red Cross nurses marching up Seventeenth Street past the Daughters of the American Revolution headquarters in 1917 as part of the ceremonies dedicating the new Red Cross headquarters. Taft presided over the ceremonies and Wilson over the review. *(LC)*

View from the old Ordnance Office at Eighteenth and E Streets looking across the Red Cross building toward the Washington Monument and downtown Washington. In the immediate foreground is the original Liberty Baptist Church. *(LC)*

The Prince of Wales visited the Red Cross in November 1919, accompanied by his staff and various officials. The prince expressed his gratitude for the Red Cross's work with its British counterpart during the war. *(LC)*

The stately Federal Reserve Eccles Building, one of a row of monumental edifices lining Constitution Avenue. Built in 1937, it was designed by Paul Phillippe Cret, who also designed the nearby Pan-American Union Building and Folger Library on Capitol Hill. *(LC)*

The Peoples Life Insurance building in the 600 block of New Hampshire Avenue was built in monumental style in the 1950s. It was sold to the government of Saudi Arabia in 1983 for that country's new embassy. *(Star)*

The west side of the Pan-American Union or International Union of the American Republics (now the Organization of American States) Building is shown here going up at Seventeenth and Constitution in January 1909. The decrepit Van Ness Mansion, abandoned for half a century, was demolished to make way for this building. *(LC)*

National and International Institutions

Here completed, the new white marble International Union of the American Republics Building sparkles. *(LC)*

The American Institute of Pharmacy Building anchored the western edge of the string of monumental buildings on Constitution Avenue. The design by John Russell Pope was one he had earlier pitched for a memorial to Lincoln in Illinois. Appropriately, today one can gaze from its steps to the Lincoln Memorial. (The 1959–62 addition to the rear led to the demolition of the Congers Laundry. That addition, in turn, has now been replaced by a much larger one, dedicated in 2009.) *(DCPL)*

Bracketing Foggy Bottom to the north are the buildings of the World Bank and International Monetary Fund (IMF), seen here with the United Church in the foreground. Originally Concordia German Evangelical, this fine Gothic Revival church, designed by Paul Schulze and Albert Goenner, was the third church structure on the site. *(Star)*

Here the new building (now demolished) for the IMF is under construction at Nineteenth and H Streets. *(Star)*

The Pan-American Health Organization also makes its home in Foggy Bottom in a curious, unique-in-Washington International-style building. Said to resemble the United Nations building in New York City, it was designed by Uruguayan Roman Fresnedo Siri and opened in 1965. *(Star)*

CHANGE

Foggy Bottom and the West End After 1950

Washington, D.C., has neighborhoods that were built at a certain time and have since remained largely unaltered. A few buildings here and there may change, but the general fabric looks much as it did in 1890, 1910 or 1940. However, Foggy Bottom and the West End have never been amongst these static enclaves. These two neighborhoods have changed drastically over the last two hundred years. They started as outgrowths from small settlements on the Potomac or more established areas to the east or west. The Chesapeake and Ohio Canal attracted more serious industry to the neighborhoods, as well as the workers to serve it. The early Federal-style homes were replaced with factories and Victorian row homes. The row homes were, in turn, replaced by small apartment buildings. The early twentieth century saw the stately houses on the eastern edge of the neighborhood taken over or torn down for offices, and even before World War II, the federal government was rapidly turning the southern portion of the neighborhood into its own.

Thus, it is inaccurate to see the dramatic changes that happened to Foggy Bottom and the West End after 1950 as putting an end to some golden era of stasis. This does not alter the fact that the change that was wrought in the postwar years was certainly on an unprecedented scale. These changes were championed by many for their benefits: improved traffic flow, the elimination of noxious industry, the opportunity to plan entire blocks at a time. But for these benefits to be realized, much of what came before had to be eliminated.

Perhaps the biggest change was in infrastructure. As in many cities in the 1950s and 1960s, planners in D.C. fell in love with roads. They devised an ambitious scheme to bring expressways right into the heart of Washington. This effort would eventually be thwarted by citizen groups, and the "Inner Loop" would never be completed. However, the portion slated for Foggy Bottom would be. This was due, in part, to the neighborhood's proximity to the new Whitehurst Freeway in Georgetown, completed in 1949, and the Theodore Roosevelt Bridge, opened in 1966. Both facilitated commutes from Northern Virginia into the downtown. With mostly just light industry and "slum" housing in its way, the E Street Expressway was able to come in off the Roosevelt Bridge, snake around Observatory Hill and send tentacles up to K Street and down five blocks of E Street itself.

Emphasizing the fact that Washington was now a city of office-bound commuters, the industrial uses that had long defined Foggy Bottom were entirely removed in the 1960s and 1970s. Interestingly, not only were the old factories demolished, but also the replacements were so grand that they entirely redefined the neighborhood. The southern ten acres of the Washington Gasworks, including the very visible storage tanks, were redeveloped into the Watergate complex. Just downriver, the Heurich Brewery site and Water Gate Inn gave way to the John F. Kennedy Center for the Performing Arts.

At the same time, the commercial area between the White House and New Hampshire Avenue filled with new office buildings. George Washington University expanded rapidly, pushing (sometimes literally, as in the case of the Lenthall Houses) older uses out of its way. Planners also turned their attention to the parking lots, car showrooms and small-scale industrial buildings of the West End. The National Capital Planning Commission (NCPC) considered turning the entire neighborhood into an international center for embassies. Then, in 1972, the city released *New Town for the West End*, which proposed high-density residential development. Private owners decided to take matters into their own hands and, led by developer Oliver T. Carr Jr., came up with their own plan for high density, mixed-use development. It called for new apartments for about forty-five hundred residents and offices for twelve thousand workers. It was adopted by the Zoning Commission in 1974 and has since been largely realized, particularly in the area around M Street and northward.

Not everyone was comfortable with the rate or scale of change in the second half of the twentieth century. Even as urban renewal surged ahead, citizens and officials acted to save portions of Foggy Bottom, like Hughes'

Alley and Snow's Court, with the result that Foggy Bottom still has alley dwellings, whereas they have been largely wiped out in much of the rest of the city. Modern architects were encouraged to design their new buildings as backdrops to the old, as in the case of the Octagon and Red Lion Row. As a result of these preservation activities, at least some portions of Foggy Bottom and the West End—neighborhoods that have never stopped changing since their earliest days—reached a point where they would not likely change much more.

The construction of the K Street Underpass beneath Washington Circle was conceived in 1938, and similar underpasses at Dupont and Scott Circles were completed in the 1940s. Construction at K Street would not begin until the summer of 1960. *(DCPL)*

Although it looks like this worker is crossing over a river, the surface below is actually the top of the underpass. *(DCPL)*

Construction of the underpass was disruptive to nearby residents and businesses, such as these along K Street, but not nearly as disruptive as the proposed K Street Expressway would have been; that change never made it off the drawing boards. *(DCPL)*

If the K Street Expressway had been built, it would have acted as an extension to the Whitehurst Freeway in Georgetown, which can be seen in the bottom right of this photo. *(Star)*

As it was, much clearing and construction was needed at the border of Foggy Bottom and Georgetown to bridge Rock Creek and connect K Street to the Rock Creek Parkway, Whitehurst Freeway and the E Street Expressway. *(LC)*

This corner of a block of I Street, complete with a street tree and two emergency call boxes, was isolated by highway construction, as shown in this 1966 photograph. *(Star)*

The E Street Expressway was intended to be part of the western leg of an "Inner Loop" freeway that was never fully built. The cars whose flow this massive project sought to ease are very much visible in all of the surface parking lots seen in this circa 1964 construction photo. *(DCPL)*

In order to do less visual damage to the federal buildings in the vicinity, the E Street Expressway was kept below-grade east of Twenty-third Street. Noted architect Chloethiel Woodard Smith designed much of the original landscaping and streetscape that surrounded and covered the cut. *(DCPL)*

Change

The Watergate complex, under construction here in 1970, was built by Italy's Societa Generale Immobiliare on land that once housed a portion of the Washington Gas Works. The Watergate name would become forever associated with political scandal as a result of the 1972 break-in to the headquarters of the Democratic Party, which was in one of the two office buildings that are part of the complex. *(Star)*

In addition to two office buildings, the Watergate development includes three cooperative apartment buildings, retail and a hotel. The curvilinear design of the buildings was intended by the architect Luigi Moretti to play off the eddy and flow of the adjacent river. *(Star)*

The Watergate was one of the first "planned unit developments" permitted under Washington's zoning code. The retail was mostly in a sunken plaza in the center of the complex. *(Star)*

A Watergate not realized: Marjorie Hendricks, proprietor of the Water Gate Inn, wanted to build this Watergate Hotel in 1960. The site would be taken by the Kennedy Center instead. *(LC)*

The John F. Kennedy Center for the Performing Arts, shown nearing completion in this 1971 photograph, was designed by architect Edward Durrell Stone. *(DCPL)*

The Kennedy Center would bring culture like the National Symphony Orchestra and Washington National Opera to Foggy Bottom (as the Washington Auditorium had once proposed to do), but would remain isolated from the neighborhood as a result of the E Street Expressway. *(Star)*

In 1955, urban renewal came to Foggy Bottom. Columbia Plaza along Virginia Avenue between the E Street Expressway and Twenty-third Street was the primary result. These 1960 models compare what could be built without and with condemnation. *(Star)*

Change

The first phase of Columbia Plaza was complete by 1967. The Keyes, Lethbridge & Condon design included apartments, duplex town homes and a hotel, all above underground parking. The hotel use was later switched to office use. *(DCPL)*

As with the Watergate, the center of Columbia Plaza included retail for the residents of the super block and any outsiders who were able to find their way in. *(Star)*

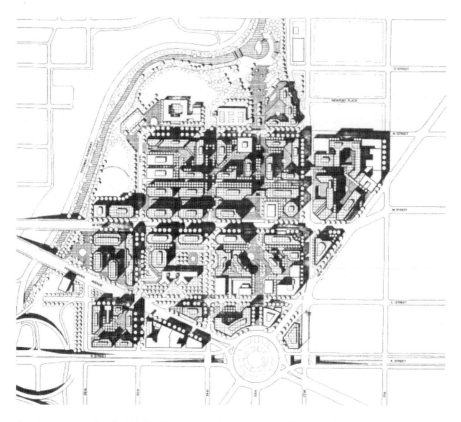

A private group, headed by Washington real estate mogul Oliver T. Carr Jr., directed architect Angelos Demetriou to produce the 1973 plan for the West End, shown here. Some of the recommendations of this plan, including public plazas and a mix of residential and commercial uses, were largely adopted, although the exact form of development would differ considerably, and the L'Enfant street network remained unchanged. *(DCPL)*

Change

A casualty of the redevelopment of the West End was the main store and headquarters of Goodwill Industries, closed in 1977 after over forty years at 1218 New Hampshire Avenue. *(Star)*

Judge Burnita Matthews owned property in Foggy Bottom on Twenty-fifth Street, across from Snow's Court. She and her brother had been early redevelopers in the neighborhood in the 1930s. She came in for criticism from the *Washington Post* in the 1950s for poor property conditions. *(Star)*

The alleys of Washington, D.C., were lamented by early twentieth-century reformers as being "shut…off from the ordinary wholesome influences and standards of life." But reformers a couple of generations later would think them worth preserving. *(Star)*

Hughes' Alley became Hughes Mews with restored houses. *(Star)*

While some of Foggy Bottom's residential architecture was preserved in the era of Modern design, commercial structures were not always as fortunate. The Lemon Building, shown here, was demolished to make way for the American Institute of Architects (AIA) headquarters in 1972. *(Star)*

The Octagon House itself was preserved. The favored approach of architects at the time was to have the new building (in this case, the AIA headquarters) inserted as a backdrop for the old. *(Star)*

This structure now has an address of 606–610 Twenty-first Street, but it was originally at Nineteenth and G Streets. It is referred to as the Lenthall Houses, after its builder, John Lenthall. For a number of years, it had been the Lenthall Home for Widows, organized by Mrs. E.J. Stone in 1883. *(LC)*

The Lenthall Houses date back to about 1800, making them some of the oldest structures in the city. They were moved on August 5, 1978, to accommodate a George Washington University project and are thus an example of one approach to preservation in the neighborhood. *(LC)*

The group of former residences and shops along I Street known as Red Lion Row, shown here in 1976, was largely preserved in place. *(LC)*

Left: The source of the Red Lion appellation is on the left. In 1982, an eight-story office and retail complex was constructed behind Red Lion Row and connected to the rear of the nineteenth-century buildings. *(LC)*

Below: Construction of the Washington Metrorail subway system began in 1969, and Foggy Bottom's station opened in 1977. In this construction photo, a portion of the tunnel sits on Virginia Avenue in August 1972; the line was being constructed underneath nearby I Street. *(Star)*

Washington, D.C.'s first monument to its namesake returns after construction of the K Street Underpass in 1962. The general, as depicted by architect-sculptor Clark Mills, remains calm in the face of change around him. The monument had been installed to great fanfare over a century earlier, dedicated on February 22, 1860. *(Star)*

Foggy Bottom and the West En[d]

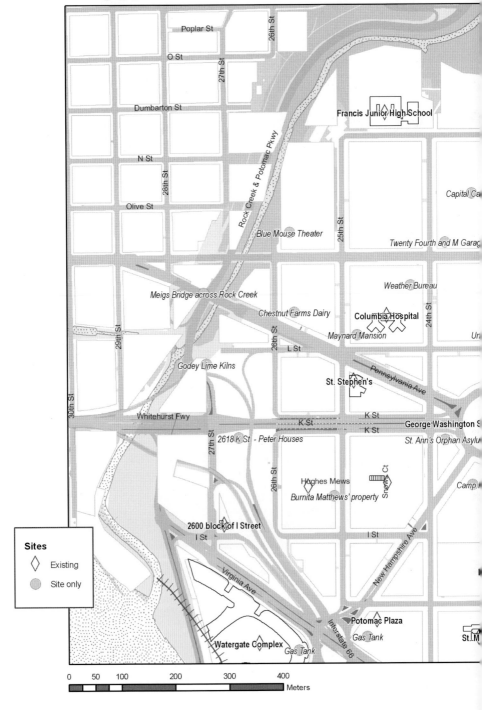

Sites

◇ Existing

◉ Site only

0 50 100 200 300 400
Meters

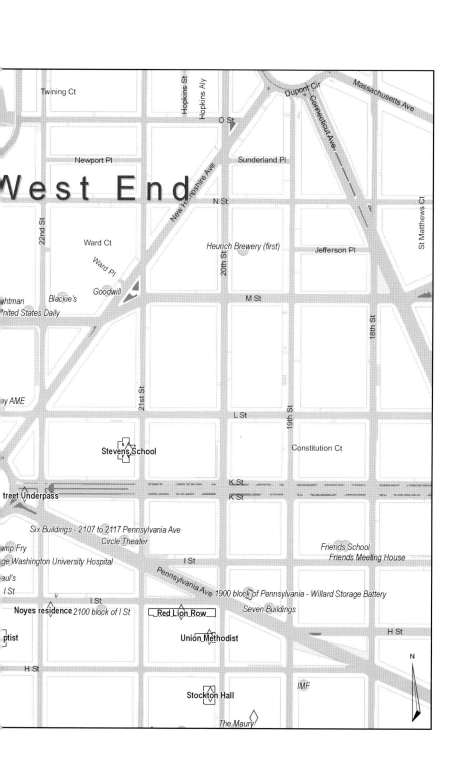

Twining Ct

Hopkins St

Hopkins Aly

Dupont Cir

Massachusetts Ave

Connecticut Ave

O St

Newport Pl

Sunderland Pl

West End

New Hampshire Ave

N St

St Matthews Ct

22nd St

Ward Ct

Heurich Brewery (first)

Jefferson Pl

20th St

Ward Pl

Goodwill

M St

18th St

...htman

Blackie's

...nited States Daily

...y AME

21st St

19th St

L St

Stevens School

Constitution Ct

K St

...treet Underpass

K St

Six Buildings - 2107 to 2117 Pennsylvania Ave

Circle Theater

...mp Fry

Friends School

...ge Washington University Hospital

Friends Meeting House

...aul's

I St

I St

Pennsylvania Ave

1900 block of Pennsylvania - Willard Storage Battery

Noyes residence

2100 block of I St

I St

Red Lion Row

Seven Buildings

H St

...ptist

Union Methodist

N

H St

IMF

Stockton Hall

The Maury

Foggy Bottom and the West En[d]

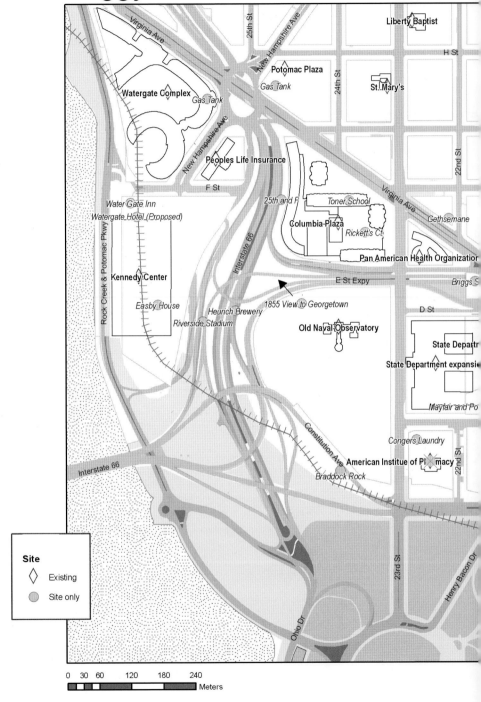

Liberty Baptist

H St

Virginia Ave

25th St

New Hampshire Ave

Potomac Plaza

Gas Tank

24th St

St. Mary's

Watergate Complex

Gas Tank

New Hampshire Ave

Peoples Life Insurance

F St

22nd St

Virginia Ave

Gethsemane

Water Gate Inn

Watergate Hotel (Proposed)

25th and F

Toner School

Rock Creek & Potomac Pkwy

Interstate 66

Columbia Plaza

Rickett's Ct

Pan American Health Organization

Kennedy Center

E St Expy

Briggs S

Easby House

1855 View to Georgetown

D St

Heurich Brewery

Riverside Stadium

Old Naval Observatory

State Departr

State Department expansi

Mayfair and Po

Congers Laundry

Interstate 66

Constitution Ave

American Institue of Pharmacy

22nd St

Braddock Rock

Ohio Dr

23rd St

Henry Bacon Dr

Site

◇ Existing

● Site only

0   30   60   120   180   240
Meters

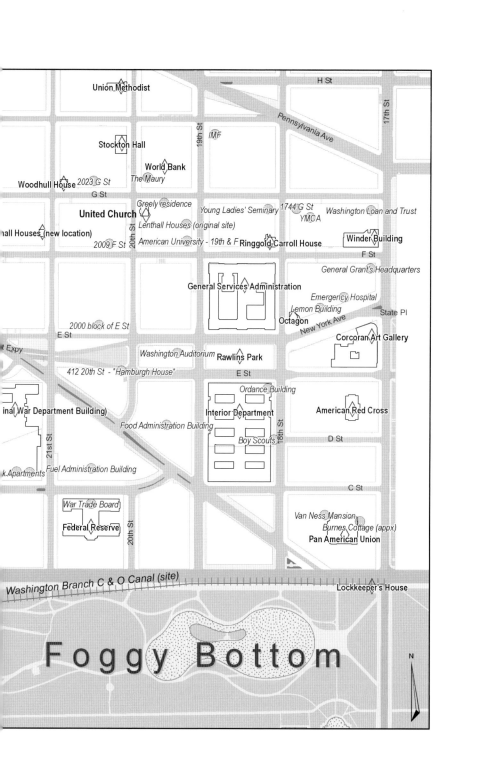

Union Methodist

Stockton Hall

H St

17th St

19th St

IMF

Pennsylvania Ave

World Bank

The Maury

Woodhull House   2023 G St

G St

Greely residence

United Church

Lenthall Houses (original site)

nall Houses (new location)

2009 F St

20th St

American University - 19th & F

Young Ladies' Seminary   1744 G St

YMCA

Washington Loan and Trust

Ringgold-Carroll House

Winder Building

F St

General Grant's Headquarters

General Services Administration

Emergency Hospital

Lemon Building

Octagon

New York Ave

State Pl

2000 block of E St

E St

Corcoran Art Gallery

Washington Auditorium   Rawlins Park

412 20th St - "Hamburgh House"

E St

Ordance Building

nal War Department Building)

Interior Department

21st St

Food Administration Building

18th St

American Red Cross

D St

Boy Scouts

k.Apartments   Fuel Administration Building

C St

War Trade Board

Van Ness Mansion

Burnes Cottage (appx)

Federal Reserve

20th St

Pan American Union

Washington Branch C & O Canal (site)

Lockkeeper's House

Foggy Bottom

N

KEY TO ILLUSTRATION SOURCES

DCPL: Washingtoniana Division, DC Public Library

HSW: The Historical Society of Washington, D.C.

LC: Library of Congress

NOAA: National Oceanic and Atmospheric Administration

SF: Sidwell Friends

Star: DC Public Library, Star Collection, copyright *Washington Post*

SELECTED BIBLIOGRAPHY

Croggon, James. "Bytes of History; Early 19th-Century Neighborhoods: The Evening Star Articles by James Croggon." http://bytesofhistory.com/Collections/Croggon/Croggon_Menu.html.

Demtreiou, Angelos C. *The West End, Washington, D.C.* Washington, D.C.: West End Planning, Oliver T. Carr Company, 1973.

Dick, Steven J. *Sky and Ocean Joined: The U.S. Naval Observatory, 1830–2000.* New York: Cambridge University Press, 2003.

Easby-Smith, Wilhelmine E. *Personal Recollections of Early Washington and a Sketch of the Life of Captain William Easby. A Paper Read before the Association of the Oldest Inhabitants of the District of Columbia, June 4, 1913.* Washington, D.C.: Association of Oldest Inhabitants, 1913.

EHT Traceries, Inc., and D.C. Preservation League. *Foggy Bottom Historic District.* Washington, D.C.: D.C. Historic Preservation Office, 2003.

Gatti, Lawrence. *Historic St. Stephen's: An Account of Its Eighty-five Years, 1867–1952.* Washington, D.C.: 1952.

Goode, James. *Best Addresses: A Century of Washington's Distinguished Apartment Houses.* Washington, D.C.: Smithsonian Books, 1988.

Herman, Jan K. *A Hilltop in Foggy Bottom: Home of the Old Naval Observatory and the Navy Medical Department.* Washington, D.C.: Naval Medical Command, Department of the Navy, 1984.

Hines, Christian. *Early Recollections of Washington City.* Washington, D.C.: Chronicle Book and Job Print, 1866.

Jones, William Henry. *Recreation and Amusement Among Negroes in Washington, D.C.* Washington, D.C.: Howard University Press, 1927.

Langley, Harold D. *St. Stephen Martyr Church and the Community, 1867–1967.* Washington, D.C.: Centennial Committee, 1968.

Mallon, Thomas. "A House in Foggy Bottom." *American Scholar* 73 (2004): 5–9.

Myer, Donald. *Bridges and the City of Washington.* Washington, D.C.: Commission of Fine Arts, 1974.

Parris, Albion Keith. "Recollections of Our Neighbors in the First Ward in the Early Sixties." *Records of the Columbia Historical Society* 29–30 (1928): 269–89.

Parsons and Versar, Inc. "The Archaeology of an Urban Landscape, the Whitehurst Freeway Archaeological Project." Report, D.C. Department of Transportation, 2006.

Scott, Pamela. "Places of Worship in the District of Columbia." Bound report, 2003.

Scott, Pamela, and Antoinette Lee. *Buildings of the District of Columbia.* New York: Oxford University Press, 1993.

Sherwood, Suzanne Berry. *Foggy Bottom 1800–1975: A Study of Uses of an Urban Neighborhood.* Washington, D.C.: Center for Washington Area Studies, 1978.

Unger, Suzanne Sherwood. "Foggy Bottom: Blue-Collar Neighborhood in a White-Collar Town." In *Washington at Home: An Illustrated History of*

Neighborhoods in the Nation's Capital. Edited by Kathryn Schneider Smith. Northridge, CA: Windsor Publications, 1988.

Weller, Charles Frederick, and Eugenia Winston Weller. *Neglected Neighbors: Stories of Life in the Alleys, Tenements, and Shanties of the National Capital.* Philadelphia: J.C. Winston, 1909.

ABOUT THE AUTHORS

Matthew Gilmore has authored a number of books: *Historic Photos of Washington, D.C.* (with Andrew Brodie Smith), *Historic Photos of Arlington County* and *Historic Photos of Franklin Delano Roosevelt.* He is the founding editor of H-DC, the Washington, D.C. history discussion list and website (http://www.h-net.org/~dclist) and has published in, guest co-edited for and serves on the editorial board of *Washington History,* the journal of the Historical Society of Washington, D.C. He is a graduate of the University of California, Los Angeles.

Josh Olsen is the author of *Better Places, Better Lives: A Biography of James Rouse,* which chronicles the rise of one of America's great city shapers. Josh is currently in charge of acquisitions for a real estate development company in Washington, D.C. He is a graduate of Yale University and earned a master's degree in geography while on a Fulbright Scholarship in the United Kingdom. Josh serves on the advisory board of H-DC.

Visit us at
www.historypress.net